One Man's Restoration

Every Aborted Baby Has A Father

by

George Curtiss

Copyright © 2012 by George Curtiss

One Man's Restoration
Every Aborted Baby Has A Father
by George Curtiss

Printed in the United States of America

ISBN 9781624190551

All rights reserved solely by the author. The author guarantees all contents are original and do not infringe upon the legal rights of any other person or work. No part of this book may be reproduced in any form without the permission of the author. The views expressed in this book are not necessarily those of the publisher.

Unless otherwise indicated, Bible quotations are taken from The King James Version (KJV); The New King James Version (NKJV). Copyright © 1991 by Thomas Nelson, Inc.; and The New International Version (NIV). Copyright © 1990 by The Zondervan Corporation.

Excerpts from the book, "6 Big, Big, Big Angels" quoted by permission of Mary Jo and Don Pennington.

Permission given by The Elijah List to quote article: "Seeing The Unseen and Hearing the Unheard and The Light Invasion of 2008"
By Patricia King, Extreme Prophetic Ministries,

Email:info@extremeprophetic.com
ElijahList Publications
www.elijahlist.com
email: info@elijahlist.net

www.xulonpress.com

Dedication

To Jesus Christ, Lord and Savior

I would like to dedicate this book to the Lord Jesus Christ.

Thank you, Jesus, for your unfailing goodness, mercy and faithfulness!

Surely goodness and mercy shall follow me all the days of my life; and I will dwell in the house of the Lord Forever. (Psalm 23:6 NKJV)

Through the Lord's mercies we are not consumed, because His compassions fail not. They are new every morning; Great is Your faithfulness." (Lamentations 3:22-23 NKJV)

Acknowledgements

"This is not a one man show." - George Curtiss

I would like to thank several people: Anne Renda, a wonderful friend the Lord put in my life, who has been a part of this book from start to finish. This book could not have been accomplished without her help.

Darlene and Howard Hunter, very good friends in the Lord, whose friendship and support were invaluable to me. It was at their lodge where I first began writing the book.

Mary Jo and Don Pennington, who allowed me to quote from their book, "6 Big, Big, Big Angels", and also encouraged me to finish writing this story and even provided the title!

Willie Richmond, another precious friend, who saw in me what I could not see in myself, and helped reveal the supernatural realm to me.

Lesley Ann Bosworth, for her gracious help and wisdom in helping put the book together.

And a very special thank you to Doris Olsen, whose gifting and anointing helped me put on paper the story

I wanted to tell. This could not have been done without her. She did an outstanding job!

Thank you, Jesus!

"From whom the whole body, joined and knit together by what every joint supplies, according to the effective working by which every part does its share, causes growth of the body for the edifying of itself in love." (Ephesians 4:16 NKJV)

"For God is not unjust to forget your work and labor of love which you have shown toward His name, in that you have ministered to the saints, and do minister." (Hebrews 6:10 NKJV)

Table of Contents

Dedication v

Acknowledgements vii

Preface xi

Introduction xiii

Chapter 1 : Sequence Of Events 15

Chapter 2 : The Year Was 1951 18

Chapter 3 : Getting The Victory 23

Chapter 4 : 2008 Year of New Beginnings 26

Chapter 5 : Till We Meet Again 29

Chapter 6 : Open Heaven 2008 37

Chapter 7 : Heavenly Realms 44

Chapter 8 : Set Free, To Set The Captives Free 49

Chapter 9 : Restoration 2009 55

Chapter 10 : Field Without Borders 58

Preface

In 2010, Howard and Darlene Hunter dedicated their "Susitna River Lodge" in Talkeetna, Alaska, to the Lord Jesus. I was invited to be part of the dedication ceremony. Afterwards, I stayed for forty days and began to write the story of how the Lord brought restoration to my life.

They say truth is stranger than fiction.

This is the true story that changed my life forever and redeemed the past 59 years.

Introduction

"Jesus did many other things as well. If every one of them were written down, I suppose that even the whole world would not have room for the books that would be written." (John 21:25 NIV)

He is still doing *many other things* and this book is my unfinished story of some of the "things" that He has done for me.

Restoration!

Chapter 1

Sequence of Events

In the spring of 2006, as I was having breakfast in a restaurant in Dallas, Oregon; a young man came and sat down at the table with me. I did not recognize him. He said he was coming up to Petersburg, Alaska to go fishing and intended to stay at my lodge, across the bay. He had found out about the lodge from my cousin, Ray, who headed up a group of men from Dallas. This group got together every year to go fishing. Bob Thomas, one of the members of the group, had become a good friend of mine over the years. In the fall, I was again in Dallas eating breakfast at the same restaurant. Bob walked in, saw me, came over and sat down with me. He asked me what had brought me south; I told him I had spent 38 winters in Alaska and that it would be a nice change to spend the winter in a hotel in Oregon.

Bob mentioned he had a travel trailer available and that it would be a lot nicer than a hotel room, if I was interested. He knew of a nice trailer park to move it to and said that I could stay there for the winter. A few days later, I called Bob and asked if the offer was still available. He said yes, and he would move the trailer to Salt Creek for me, a few miles away from Dallas. When I was settled into the trailer, I phoned Bob to talk to him, but he was not at home. I went to the restaurant to see if he was there. He wasn't there either, so I sat down at a table with a cup of coffee to figure out what to do next. I noticed the man at the next table kept glancing at me as if he recognized me, so I gave him a good look back. There next to him, sat my cousin Ray's sister, Millie, whom I had not seen for years, and her husband, Dick. After we greeted each other, they wanted to know what had brought me here. I told them the story about running into my friend Bob, and that I was going to be living in his travel trailer at Salt Creek for the winter. "What a small world," Millie said. "We live in a trailer park nearby. When you get settled come by and see us."

Soon afterward, I called Millie. After her first husband had died, she married Dick, whose wife had also died. They had not been married very long. We had a lot of catching up to do. As we talked, the conversation got around to where I was living. I told them it was a very large park, with Salt Creek bordering the rear of the property. There was a bridge that crossed the creek to a field with a house on it. I could see people moving about, but it was too far away to identify anyone. Millie then told me that Dick had built that house and had sold it to a friend, John Smith. When she told me that, my heart skipped a beat or two, because I knew that John had married Betty, a woman whom I had a previous relationship with! I was then told that they not only owned the field across the creek from me, but also the land the trailer was on.

Sequence Of Events

What I am about to describe next, is something that started a sequence of events that changed my life forever. One evening, soon after I had moved into the trailer, I was watching a true story about a man's life on television. He was raised in a caring, loving family. They were devout Catholics. He was an altar boy planning on becoming a priest, when his priest began sexually abusing him.

He started to change from being a well-adjusted boy to being withdrawn, untrustworthy and fearful. He did not tell his parents what the priest was doing to him, because the boy thought it was his fault. As he grew older, he became rebellious with his parents, school and religion. He quit being an altar boy and the church altogether. In his late fifties, he had become a bitter old man. His brother became very worried what would become of him. He confided in his brother and realized the root of his problem - that of being sexually abused as a child. He had never told anyone about the abuse, until that moment.

Seeing this true story had a very strong affect on me, because I too, had become a bitter old man. I, too, had secrets from my past, that I had never told anyone about. I had never had told anyone about the problems Betty and I faced in our past relationship. The secrets had caused great bitterness between us. (Hebrews 12:15 NIV) described my life: *See to it that no one falls short of the grace of God and that no bitter root grows up to cause trouble and defile many.*

Chapter 2

The Year Was 1951

I was attending high school in Dallas, Oregon. I was a sophomore playing on the football team. We had taken first place in our league, which qualified us to advance to the next level of play, on our way to becoming state champions.

We had won the quarter final game and were playing in the semi-finals against Milton-Freewater High in Eastern, Oregon. Sitting in the stands at that semi-final football game was a young woman, named Betty. It was at this game that I had caught her eye. We were beaten in that game and eliminated from becoming state champions. It was also the beginning of being defeated in my life's journey! With the loss of that game, football season ended. The next thing on my agenda was basketball.

One evening, as I was walking home after basketball practice, a black Oldsmobile pulled up beside me. The young woman behind the wheel rolled down the window and asked if I would like a ride home. I gratefully accepted her offer. On our way home she asked if I knew how to dance and if I would like to learn. I said, "Sure." So, instead of going home we went out dancing.

The Year Was 1951

This was the beginning of a very unusual relationship. Betty was seven years old than me, she still lived at home, and most of her friends were already married. We were a couple throughout my high school years at times it was awkward because of the age difference.

During my junior year, Betty told me that she was pregnant. She found a doctor who would perform an abortion. It was performed on a dark stormy, winter night. It was all very secretive, because having an abortion was against the law at the time; both the doctor and patient could be arrested. I don't remember much about it. No one talked about it afterwards. I told no one. It was a dark time in our lives. I probably felt relieved, although my thoughts were always accusing me and I was always trying to defend the actions taken.

Who show the work of the law written in their hearts, their conscience also bearing witness, and between themselves their thoughts accusing or else excusing them in the day when God will judge the secrets of men by Jesus Christ, according to my gospel. (Romans 2:15-16 NKJV)

This truly affected me. I knew it was wrong, but once you taste the lust of the flesh, it is a very strong impulse. (It is how the Lord sustains the human race.) You see, God has a beautiful plan, a profound mystery called marriage; where a man and a woman become one.

Because I didn't understand His plan, "...my people perish for lack of knowledge." (See Hosea 4:6 KJV) I tasted and enjoyed the fruit of the flesh and became in bondage to it.

Do not be deceived, God cannot be mocked. A man reaps what he sows. The one that sows in the flesh, will reap in the flesh. (Galatians 6:7-8 NKJV)

At this time, the United States was engaged in the Korean Conflict. At the age of 19, every male would get a draft notice from "Uncle Sam" telling them they had to join the army for active service. The only way one could be exempt from the draft was to join another service, go to college, become a conscientious objector, or have health reasons.

I had received two college scholarships to play football that fall and had chosen Oregon College of Education in Monmouth, Oregon. I became engaged to marry Betty and joined the Navy Reserves. I had my life all planned out for the next four years. What I hadn't planned for was Betty getting pregnant again.

This changed all my plans. I now had a responsibility to Betty and the baby. We got a marriage license, bought wedding rings, and I returned the football equipment for the fall season. I dropped out, before I even started because I wanted to get my draft obligation over as soon as possible. I quit the Naval Reserves and enlisted in the Marines.

Now listen, you who say, "Today or tomorrow we will go to this or that city, spend a year there, carry on business and make money."

Why, you do not even know what will happen tomorrow. What is your life? You are a mist that appears for a little while and then vanishes. Instead, you ought to say, "If it is the Lord's will, we will live and do this or that." (James 4:13-15 NIV)

The recruiting officer advised me that I should wait until I got out of boot camp before getting married. He said that I would get 15 days leave before being shipped out to Korea.

I don't know how to describe boot camp. It was the longest three months of my life. It was not only physical training but also mental anguish. It was hell on earth. I could hardly wait for it to be over. That day finally arrived and I was on my way home. I found out that Betty had gotten yet another abortion and my world was shattered. I was devastated. I had no idea how these chains of events would affected me throughout my whole life.

I did not realize it until I saw the movie on television about the altar boy who was sexually molested. The Lord used this movie to break my heart of stone. He brought back memories that I had buried over 50 years ago. I had been in bondage that long, never telling anyone about the abortions, and hardly even remembering them myself.

Holy Spirit brought back to my remembrance (Paraphrase, James 5:16 NKJV): *Therefore, confess your sins to each other and pray for one another so that you may be <u>healed.</u>*

I knew if I didn't confess this right then, that I'd never do it. It had been buried for so long, that it became a very strong wall around my heart. It would take a miracle to knock it down.

Then you will know the Truth and the Truth will set you free. So if the Son sets you free, you will be free indeed. (Paraphrase, John 8:32, 36 NKJV)

And Jesus has set me free!

Chapter 3

Getting The Victory

This has been the most difficult chapter for me to write. It was hard for me to understand what the Lord was doing with me. He brought back memories that had been buried since 1953. My emotions then were those of anger and frustration. Being ignorant in the ways of the Lord, I did not understand how anger can affect one's life journey. Dealing with anger is a key in the process of healing.

Be angry and do not sin. Do not let the sun go down on your wrath. (Ephesians 4:26 NKJV)

I had so many "sun sets" on my anger that had never been dealt with, but needed to be, before I could be set free. This made the next few years very interesting. I had taken the first step and confessed the secret. Memories that had been lost since 1953, came flooding back.

I remember when I was flying home from boot camp to get married to Betty. It was so real to me, like it was yesterday. I could see the city of Portland below as the plane banked over the Columbia River to land at the airport. I was so excited to see Betty. I could even remember what she wore. She was wearing a jacket made of small colored squares; red, orange, yellow and green. Her hair was auburn and she stood out like a spring flower. As we drove back to Dallas, I realized Betty did not look pregnant anymore. She informed me that she had had another abortion. I did not handle the news very well. All that I had gone through in the past months; all I had given up for her and the baby, was suddenly diminished by an "inconvenience". I didn't know whether to weep or give in to my anger, my emotions were in turmoil.

I borrowed my dad's car to take a drive and cool down, but began drinking instead. I arrived drunk at Betty's home and after a heated argument with her, proceeded to her backyard where I threw my wedding ring as far as I could throw it. I got back into the car, put the pedal to the metal and ran two stop lights on my way out of town, missing a turn in the road and rolling dad's car over and over, clear across a bridge and ending upside down. I ran away from the scene of that accident and considered myself lucky to have survived it. God had other plans for me!

Just last year, I was talking to my younger brother, Jerry, about the things that happened the night of that accident. He added something he recollected. He was five years old and remembers me sitting hunched over and upset next to the oil stove in our living room. He knew I was angry because when he tried to speak to me, I turned around, glared at him, and for no reason gave him a gesture with my middle finger. Can you imagine how this made me feel when he told me that?

It broke my heart and I asked Jerry to forgive me. He replied, "George, it's no big deal." I said, "Jerry it was a huge deal, especially if you still remember after all these years. What kind of an impression for an older brother to leave on your younger brother's life." With tears in my eyes, I gave Jerry a big hug. The Lord used this to give me victory over another root of anger that I had let the sun set on.

At this point I was starting to understand that the Lord had brought these memories back to my remembrance for a purpose. They needed to be dealt with. It was a process that He was using to deliver me from all the strongholds that the evil one had used to defeat me.

He was showing me *"the battle is the Lord's"* (See 2 Chronicles 20:15) and He was giving me the victory. This was a huge revelation to me. I am big man, a football player, a Marine, a John Wayne fan; *"The bigger they are, the harder they fall"*. I had always defended myself, I always retaliated. But when I read (1 Peter 2:23 NKJV); when they hurled insults at Jesus, He did not retaliate; When *He suffered, He did not threaten, but committed Himself to Him who judges righteously*

And Jesus won the final victory.

Chapter 4

2008 Year of New Beginnings

During the time that I was living in the trailer across the creek from Betty in 2007, I started attending the Jesus Pursuit Church in Albany. The church was a short drive from Salt Creek and I was really enjoying my time spent there. On Sunday, November 4th, the church bulletin announced The Elijah List Conference, "What is God Saying for 2008? Register today!" With all that had happened to me this past year, I knew I needed a touch from the Lord. I registered that day; I was excited to see what God was saying for 2008.

My prayer was (James 1:5-6 NKJV): *If any of you lacks wisdom, let him ask of God, who gives to all liberally and without reproach, and it will be given to him. But let him ask in faith...*

I went to every session and drank in every word at the conference. Each speaker's message flowed in unity. The Holy Spirit within me agreed with the word being spoken - the year 2008 was going to be a year of new beginnings! I was overwhelmed with gratitude to Jesus, for His assurance of His Word. He is faithful to His Word.

What time of blessing! I was spoken over by a number of people at the conference. One woman came up to me and asked "if I was a fisherman?" (I have lived in a fishing village in Alaska and had many fishing stories.) She "saw" me fishing with a bobber and the Lord had me in His grasp as I grasped a fishing pole with a fish on the line. I could identify with this, as I had caught a king Salmon that took first place in a fishing derby. It was the biggest fish that had been entered in seventeen years. It was worth $6,000!

Another spoke over me and said, "I 'see' you as a sweetheart. You are the Lord's sweetheart." With that word, the tears began to flow and I had to excuse myself. All the favor I was receiving there had touched my heart so. The Lord, by His goodness and love was turning my heart of stone into a heart of flesh through the people He used to speak over me.

And another said, "I 'see' you with stories. Stories that the Lord will use to bring others to Him." This has become a profound word to me, as the Lord has given me many stories since then. Stories that the Lord has used. I will include one in the next chapter, a letter that I wrote to my friend Bill, who was on my old football team.

The Lord touched me, gave me wisdom that brought healing to my heart and renewed my mind.

That you put off, concerning your former conduct, the old man which grows corrupt according to the deceitful lusts, and be renewed in the spirit of your mind, and that you put on the new man which was created according to God, in true righteousness and holiness. (Paraphrase, Ephesians 4:22-24 NKJV)

Chapter 5

Till We Meet Again

Dear Bill,

I had a dream about you last night. I don't remember what it was, but as I lay in bed trying to remember it, my thoughts went back to when we were in high school.

I recalled when you, Larry, Bruce and I were all "weigh up boys" for the summer at the farm in Independence. We all worked together harvesting beans and hops. You drove us to work in your dad's car; I believe it was a Dodge? That was a great summer! I've a lot of good memories of that time.

Then my thoughts turned to the present. We had all gone our separate ways. You and I kind of kept in touch over the years, but I didn't have any idea what had happened to Larry or Bruce until after I retired.

When I moved back to Oregon, I became re-acquainted with Larry and started going steelhead fishing with him at the places we used to fish as kids. On one of these trips, Larry asked me a question, "George, I heard that you had been a preacher at one time and I cannot believe it. I need to hear about this from the horse's mouth." I told him it was true, that I had gone to Bible School and preached at a chapel on the coast. He said, "What did you do that for? Did you need the money?" I laughed and said, "No", that I never even passed the offering plate. He then warned me, "I don't want you pushing religion down my throat." I assured him that I didn't do that either.

Over the next few years, we got together many times. He was very interested in getting us all together and bringing out the old scrap books, remembering our exploits in high school football. During this time, Larry developed bone cancer and I saw him deteriorate right before my eyes.

I was been able to share the Good News of the gospel with him during one of our fishing trips. I explained to him that it was about a personal relationship with Jesus, not a building or denomination. That it did not cost him anything to receive the free gift of what Jesus had done. I told him that he didn't need me, he could pray at anytime and anyplace. All he had to do was just thank the Heavenly Father for His great sacrifice, and when He knocks on the door of your heart, to let Him in.

One evening, Larry and his wife, Nancy came to our home for dinner. Later on in the evening Nancy played the organ for us and sang the "Old Rugged Cross". I thought the song "Amazing Grace" was more appropriate and I was making my opinion known. Larry turned to me and said, "George, why don't you quit your complaining and get over here and sing with us!"

Larry continued to get worse until he was finally hospitalized. I stopped by to see him one day and was shocked at his condition. The shades were pulled; he had tubes in his nose and arm, and had drifted into a comatose state. I sat down beside him, not knowing what to do. A nurse came in to check on him. She told me that Larry had been in a coma for a few days and that his body was slowly shutting down; but his heart was so strong that it would not let him go. She said that people in the United States just did not understand death. She said that the last thing that goes is our hearing. When a person is near death is when they need someone the most and is often when we let them down.

I thanked her for the information and mentioned that I had to leave to take care of some business, but that I would be back. When I returned a short time later, the nurse had shaved Larry, the blinds were up, the sun was shining on the flowers that someone had sent him. I spent the rest of the afternoon holding Larry's hand and talking to him.

The nurse came in, took Larry's other hand and said, "Larry, this is my long weekend off. When I come back, I don't want you to be here. You have been a good husband, a good father and you have had a good life. It's okay to go." She then left. I thought that this would be also a good time for me to leave.

One Man's Restoration

I had played football with Larry in high school. He was our quarterback, and I was the fullback. I was in the running of making the most touchdowns in the league that season, but the game is not about one person, but about the team and about winning as a team. On the last game of the season, we had the ball on the other team's 13-yard line. In the huddle, Larry mentioned that I needed points and he was calling the play. I suggested an "end-around" play where a lineman would pull off the line, and the end and halfback would run interference for me. It is not in the play books for the quarterback to run interference. His position is too valuable to risk him getting hurt. Besides, Larry was not a very big guy in high school.

We broke huddle and began the play, but the other team blocked us so Larry took the ball from the center, and pitched the ball back to me. Then he ran interference by running in front of me. I never forgot the play. I can still see Larry running and throwing a block for me. I made that touchdown. I received the most points in the league that year and made All-Star.

With Larry's hand in mine I said, "Larry, I am going now, why don't you go home and be with Jesus. You are again running interference for me and I am right behind you." He squeezed my hand and I knew in my spirit that he knew what I was talking about. Thirty minutes later, I arrived home and received a phone call that Larry had passed on.

The two songs performed at Larry's funeral were "The Old Rugged Cross" and "Amazing Grace". With tears of joy, I knew that these songs were for me because Larry was no longer down here, but at home with Jesus. I knew that I would see him again.

Bruce was at Larry's funeral. It was good to see him. We had not seen each other in years. We agreed we needed to get re-acquainted but I ended up moving back to Alaska before we got to see each other, and soon lost touch again.

Several years later, I just happened to be down in Oregon, when I got a urgent call from another old friend, Chuck, telling me that Bruce was dying of cancer and did not have long to live. He said that Bruce was in great deal of pain, and he was kept heavily sedated and slept most of the time. Chuck said Bruce was confined to his bed, and the family was not allowing visitors. I said I would like to see him anyway; he gave me directions, the phone number and wished me luck. When I called, Bruce's daughter answered. I explained I was an old high school friend and was only in the area for a short time and would like to see him. She told me she would check to see if this was possible and would get back to me. Bruce had to be prepared for the visit by reducing his medication so he would be awake. When she called back, she said it would be okay. We agreed on a time for the next day.

As I drove to Bruce's home, I had no idea what to expect. I had never met Bruce's wife or family; I didn't even know their names. I had asked the Lord to prepare the way for me because I no longer believed in luck. I was met at the front door by Bruce's wife. She told me that Bruce had wanted his old high school annuals to look at. He had been showing her pictures of me and was very excited to see me. I was shown into the room. I don't know how to describe the moment. It was like we were transported back in time.

He was sitting up in bed with his annual spread out before him. We were again, "weigh-up boys", teammates on the football field, back in boot camp in the Marine Corp. We sat and reminisced, we laughed and cried. We truly enjoyed our last moments together. We had great memories. Where did the years go? They went so fast.

I was brought back to the present time by Bruce's pain and exhaustion. I could see that he was uncomfortable and that our visit was coming to a close. I asked Bruce if he knew Jesus, if he had eternal life. He said, "No."

I then told him the story about Larry; how he had called the play in the huddle for me and then ran interference for me that game, and how Larry had squeezed my hand when I had told him that he was again running interference for me. Shortly after my visit, Larry went home to be with Jesus.

I knew Bruce would identify with this story, because he was there in the huddle as the halfback, and he also had ran interference for me. I asked Bruce if he would like to meet Jesus, that Jesus really loved him and that *these things were written so that you may KNOW that you have eternal life.* (Paraphrase, 1 John 5:13 NKJV)

I had the privilege that day of introducing Bruce to Jesus. I quoted (Paraphrase, John 3:16, 17 NKJV) to him, *For God so loved the world that He gave His only begotten Son, that whoever believes in him will not perish, but have everlasting life. God did not send His Son into the world to condemn it, but to save it.*

Bruce thanked God for Jesus. He asked Him for forgiveness for his sin and for not seeking Him earlier. He received Jesus as his Lord and Savior. With tears in our eyes, we embraced. I shared with Bruce that with that act of faith, his name was written in the Lamb's Book of Life, that all of heaven was rejoicing with us and that Jesus' Spirit came to give his spirit life. He had become born again.

It was time for me to go. I gave Bruce a big hug and said we are not only friends but now we were brothers. We never have to say good-bye again, only "until we meet again".

And with that, I left.

As I drove away, I thanked the Lord for preparing the way, for making it so simple, that a child can receive His gift and for the privilege of being a part of it. He had given me a pearl that I will cherish the rest of my life.

As I end this letter Bill, my spirit man is very tender. My prayer is that the Holy Spirit will woo you into this relationship with Jesus. You are the last one left on the team. I don't know if there will be hops and beans and football up there, but I do know it will not be the same there without you.

Your Friend,

George

(Bill called me after he received the letter and said, "You don't have to worry about me anymore, George".)

Chapter 6

Open Heaven 2008

I looked forward to the New Year in 2008 with great expectation. I could only imagine what this "Year of New Beginnings" would bring forth.

Again, I was at the Jesus Pursuit Church in Albany, OR. In the announcement was another conference, "The Ministry of Angels" scheduled for February. It read, "Vision for this conference: We are very excited to host this conference, which I believe will turn out to be an encounter with the Lord and heaven. It's my hope and prayer that those who come, will come not just out of fascination or curiosity but to join us in one heart and one mind to ask God for a greater understanding and release of His heavenly host to help the body of Christ in our region push through to breakthrough and move out into the fields that are white for harvest." I registered that day! Denny Cline, pastor of JPC, told the congregation that we worship God, we do not worship angels. *"Are they not all ministering spirits sent forth to minister for those who will inherit salvation?"* (Hebrews 1:14 NKJV)

When the conference got under way I was deeply touched by the very presence of the Lord. I saw that, *He inhabits the praises of His people* (Paraphrase, Psalm

22:3: KJV). I desired another touch from Jesus. *Delight thyself also in the Lord: and he shall give thee the desires of your heart.* (Psalm 37:4 NKJV) The Lord used Kelry Green to give me that touch. One touch so powerful that it inspired me to write this book. Kelry is Brazilian. In 2001, she had a powerful encounter with Jesus that changed the course of her life. She experienced the fire of God's Holiness and the Fear of the Lord, which caused her to lay down everything for the sake of His love.

She had brought a young Brazilian man with her, a musician who could not speak English. Kelry interpreted for him. He said that he had asked the Lord to anoint his music like He had done for King David. He played the saxophone at this conference. He would just play and play, not a specific song, but a new song. I had never heard anything like it before.

In one of Kelry's sessions, the Holy Spirit used her to rebuke the church in America. It was in Jesus' Spirit because it was done gently. She said, "You have all the conferences, all the five-fold ministries, all the tapes, DVD's, books... we had everything we needed to believe, but you still do not believe."

Our job is to believe.

The Lord used this word for me. He showed me I did not even believe! He showed me that I carry around my worries and concerns; the sin of unbelief. I repented and asked for help with my unbelief.

Casting all your care upon Him, for He cares for you. (1 Peter 5:7 NKJV)

Cast your burden on the Lord, And He shall sustain you; He shall never permit the righteous to be moved. (Psalm 55:22 NKJV)

There were two chairs on the left side in the very front. I got the outside one and a woman from Manning, Oregon, had the other one. Since we arrived so early, we had time to get acquainted. Before I knew it, the music had started. The worship service was extraordinary! The presence of the Lord was there.

Kelry said, "It's an open heaven, shut your eyes, and go there." It was opened when the veil was ripped in two.

*Then the **veil** of the temple was torn **in two** from top to bottom.* Mark 15:38 (NKJ)

I didn't understand the term "open heaven" at that time. I wanted to go there and asked the Lord if this was possible, because I wanted everything that He created for me. I closed my eyes and had a vision of a field without borders. It was full of color, flowers, butterflies, birds, rainbows and children. The children were of all colors, sizes and ages. I was not actually there; I was looking from outside the scene. The children were just delighted, they were laughing, running, jumping, twirling, playing with each other and completely enjoying themselves.

I thought, "I wonder what this event is all about?" Then I heard the Holy Spirit say to me, "Those are all the aborted babies in the time of the Millennium. They will have the best childhood of any child, because it will take a hundred years to grow up."

The Millennium is a thousand year reign of Jesus on earth, when Satan is bound and cast into the bottomless pit for a season: *"He laid hold of the dragon, that serpent of old, who is the Devil and Satan, and bound him for a thousand years; and he cast him into the bottomless pit, and shut him up, and set a seal on him, so that he should deceive the nations no more till the thousand years were finished. But after these things he must be released for a little while."* (Revelation 20:2, 3 NKJV)

I have never read or heard anyone speaking about aborted babies in the Millennium. It caused me to search the scriptures for some answers. What I found was the key that lead to the writing of this book! I cannot put into words what happened to me at that conference. It reminded me of Paul's experience, *And I know such a man—whether in the body or out of the body I do not know, God knows.* (2 Corinthians 12:3 NKJV)

It will be the time when children will have the time of their lives, because Satan will no longer interfere with them. *Never again will there be in it an infant who lives but a few days, or an old man who does not live out his years; the one who dies at a hundred will be thought a mere child.* (Isaiah 65:20 NIV)

The wolf will live with the lamb, the leopard will lie down with the goat, the calf and the lion and the yearling together; and a little child will lead them. The cow will feed with the bear, their young will lie down together, and the lion will eat straw like the ox. The infant will play near the cobra's den, and the young child will put its hand into the viper's nest. (Isaiah 11:6-8 NIV)

(Isaiah 57:1-2 NIV) tells why the young die before their time; *The righteous perish, and no one takes it to heart; the devout are taken away, and no one understands that the righteous are taken away to be spared from evil. Those who walk uprightly enter into peace; they find rest as they lie in death.* Many of the aborted babies had no future here on earth, because of their circumstances; their lives were spared from evil.

And he said, "While the child was alive, I fasted and wept; for I said, 'Who can tell whether the Lord will be gracious to me, that the child may live?' But now he is dead; why should I fast? Can I bring him back again? I shall go to him, but he shall not return to me." (2 Samuel 12:22-23 NKJV)

It is no wonder why Jesus said, *Let the little children come to me, and do not hinder them, for the kingdom of God belongs to such as these. Truly I tell you, anyone who will not receive the kingdom of God like a little child will never enter it.* (Mark 10:14-15 NIV)

I heard the saxophone come off the stage and move up and down the aisles. The saxophone player never stopped playing the whole time, even when he stood in front of me and put his hand on my shoulder. It was SO powerful, that I reached out to embrace him.

Later, the woman sitting next to me said she had never experienced anything like it before and all she could do is weep. She said, "It was if the Lord was using the young man with the anointed saxophone to minister to you, and the Lord was using you to minister to him."

The day after the conference was a beautiful, bright, spring day. I had gotten a letter from my friend, Darlene, in Talkeetna, Alaska. I found a bench to sit on and opened the letter. Inside, she had sent me an article from "The Elijah List".

Seeing The Unseen and Hearing The Unheard and The Light Invasion of 2008 by Patricia King

Be on the alert of My Sudden visitation of revelation. My messengers have been sent out from heaven with a message for you, a calling of deep unto deep. I will appear in unexpected ways. Be neither surprised nor alarmed. In this visitation, I will reveal that which you have not seen and will cause sounds you have not heard.

Do not expect the grandiose, there shall be no empire building for yourself. All this is ultimately for my purpose. If you obey my voice and my word, my reward for your pinpoint obedience will be great. Seeing the unseen and hearing the unheard.

The article went on to say:

Do not be shocked to find I am choosing a variety of vessels to manifest my light. Some will say, look at this one, he is an eccentric vessel. He operates differently from the status quo. How could this one be a true disciple of God?

Do not be surprised to find that the way these vessels release and proclaim My light are not conventional, for I am choosing a diverse way to release and proclaim My light into the earth. But you will know my chosen vessels by the Spirit. I am doing a new thing. He who has an ear to hear, let him hear.

I will use a variety of vessels! Conservative vessels, highly educated vessels, simple vessels, favored vessels, misunderstood vessels, child vessels, female vessels, male vessels, old vessels, young vessels and even vessels that do not know I am the very light they are proclaiming.

Can you fathom what I thought after reading this article and what had just happened at the Ministry of Angels Conference? I thought of the people that had ministered to me. I also prayed, "Lord, could I be one of those "vessels"?

Chapter 7

Heavenly Realms

Anne Renda is a very dear friend of mine. She is a sister in the Lord. I have known her over 14 years. We are able to share many God things together. I had shared all the things that the Lord had done at the Ministry of Angels Conference in February.

Anne was watching Sid Roth's TV program "It's Supernatural". He was interviewing Mary Jo Pennington, the author of the book, "6 Big, Big, Big Angels". Knowing that my birthday was coming up, Anne bought me the book.

Once I started reading, I could not put it down. Why don't you join me?

The book is about a visit to heaven by a 4 1/2 year old girl named "Victoria". She was visiting her grandparents. They were all in the backyard swimming pool. Her grandma was standing at the top of the slide ready to slide into the pool. Victoria asked Mary Jo, her grandmother whom she calls "Majo", "can I come up there and slide down with you?" Mary Jo, turned and looked down at her granddaughter on the pool deck below and said, "sure!"

Suddenly Majo's knees let go, her feet slid and she fell bottom first. Her backside hit Victoria who had quickly scooted up to stand directly behind her grandmother. The force of the blow knocked Victoria backwards to the concrete deck below.

The following is a description of what Grandpa Don witnessed: I am an engineer and what I saw just could not be happening. I saw Victoria propelled backward off the slide with such force that her body stretched out almost horizontal. Then I saw her body rotate (in this flat position) 180 degrees in the air. Her head was pointed at the slide and her feet were pointed in the opposite direction from how she started to fall.

She was unhurt and over time she began to tell us what had happened, "I heard God yell, 'save the children, catch Victoria.' And then 6 Big, Big, Big Angels they catch me, and zoom-they took me right up to heaven." When Victoria told us this, we were astonished. We were speechless. When we realized that was what had happened, we started asking her questions about the experience. The stories she told us over a two-year period is what led to the writing of this book.

You will realize that there are no limits in God, by faith. God and His angelic hosts are at our disposal and for our protection.

I believe that the move of God that the Holy Spirit is releasing into the earth in this day and hour is a revelation to see heavenly things and become familiar with the heavenly realms. Heaven is coming down upon us and we are being caught up into that great cloud of Glory. Allow the Holy Spirit to stretch your faith, that you too might become aware of the hosts of angels around you.

After Victoria's fall, she told her mother, "The 6 Big, Big, Big Angels, they catch me so I wouldn't crack my head. They took me right to heaven. There was a stairway to heaven and there were angels all the way to heaven! Psalm 91:12

Victoria was again at her grandparents home, Mary Jo had a set of figurines that comprised a group of musicians playing various instruments. Victoria pointed to one that was playing a saxophone.

Victoria said, "Majo, I want you to write this down cause I'm only going to tell you one time." She saw a teenage boy. He was working on writing a song. The teenage boy and Jesus asked Victoria to help them fix the instrument. After the teenage boy let her help them fix the instrument, he continued to write his song with Jesus helping him. The teenage boy then sat and played beautiful music on his saxophone.

It reminded me immediately of the young man from Brazil who had asked the Lord to anoint his music like King David, who played a new song.

I read on:

Victoria's description of heavenly fireworks: When Jesus started to approach God's throne, the big rainbow that surrounded Him touched the huge rainbow surrounding God. They merged with sparks, sparkling and twinkling like colorful fireworks. More brilliant than anything that could be described.

Again I was awed by what I read. I had a hard time realizing eternity. I knew it meant forever and ever, but

I just couldn't grasp it. I remember hearing a teacher speak on the subject. She said that eternity was like a circle. There is no beginning, no ending.

One day while flying back to Alaska, we were above the clouds. I looked out the window and saw two rainbows. They were circles, a smaller one inside a larger one. I had never heard of a round rainbow, let alone seen one! We all know what a rainbow represents; a promise that God would not destroy the earth again, by a flood. These two rainbows were like a promise to me, that I had eternal life. It became a precious pearl to me.

I told a number of people of seeing a round rainbow. One said, "I believe I heard that there is a rainbow in the "Throne Room". I said, "I bet it is round." At the Angel Conference in Albany, Kelly the lady from Brazil, asked us to open our Bible to Revelation 4:3. She read, *"And the one who sat there had the appearance of jasper and carnelian, a rainbow resembling an emerald, encircled the throne."* (Revelation 4:3 NIV) I believe the Holy Spirit put that verse in her heart just for me. I have sold fireworks for over twenty years. I am known as the Fireworks Man. I know a lot about sparks, sparkling and twinkling!

Do you think I could put the book down now, at this point? I knew this was from the Lord. Let me share one of the most powerful chapters, to me of that book:

Cemetery of the Innocents

Mary Jo wrote: "I believe one of the main reasons that God allowed Victoria to come back to us, is to tell us the truth about the aborted babies. This revelation startled me. This secret had been covered over with scars so deep it was not part of my conscience thought. ...Now the memories came flooding back. God knew my healing was not complete.

...I could never feel worthy of God's love. Every time I came before Him in prayer, I would beg Him to forgive me for the sins I had committed and for the awful life I had lived. I did not even know why I felt so unworthy. I knew Jesus' blood was sufficient, but I could not quite accept that He loved me."

One man said to me with tears rolling down his face, "They never ask the fathers. They aborted my baby without even asking me."

Chapter 8

Set Free, To Set The Captives Free

The last chapter of that book impacted me the most. I just could not stop thinking about it. Mary Jo had shared the skeleton in her closet and because I had the same experience, her words kept playing over and over in my mind. The evil one had used shame to defeat me for so long. But the year 2008, was truly my year of "New Beginnings". Thank you, Jesus!

I did not have a clue what was next on this road I was traveling. However, I did know I needed to order more of these books. I knew others that had had abortions and they too, needed to hear the good news of aborted babies in heaven. Victoria said, "The babies love their mothers and have forgiven them, they can hardly wait to see them in heaven!" What grace!

Anne gave me Mary Jo's phone number. I called and talked to her. I told her my story and how much the Lord had used her book to put light on my past life. She told me that a group in Montana had asked her to come for a week of meetings to share her book with them. She then asked me if I would like to go with her and Victoria. It didn't take long for me to decide to go!

The plan was to first meet in Whitefish, Montana. The next morning we would board the train and arrive in Chinook that afternoon. Victoria, now 11 years old, had never seen snow before. She was hoping she would see some, since we were going through the Rocky Mountains. However, in May it would normally be gone. It started to snow! Then over the sound system Christmas music started to play, I knew we were on the right track.

This was cowboy country, ranches with "fields without borders". We had a free day and the plan was to show Victoria cows and horses; the cowgirl way of life.

We rented a car and started to pull out of the driveway to follow the caravan to a potluck dinner at a nearby ranch. Mary Jo and a good friend of mine, Willie Richmond, jumped in the back seat. Anne was driving and I was sitting in the passenger seat.

A short time later, Willie put her hand on my shoulder and said, "George, shut your eyes." I just stared at her. Again, she said, "George, shut your eyes. There is a staircase going to heaven. Do you see it? Go there and quit thinking."

"Jesus is at the top of the stairs, do you see Him, George? Jesus is bidding you to come! Go George, hurry! Go to Him, He is holding your baby. Do you see George? Jesus is holding your baby to you. George, is it a boy or girl? Quit thinking."

I said, "It's a girl, I thought it was a boy." Willie said, "Oh, that's a man thing. Name her, George." I said, "Her name is Merry."

Trust in the Lord with all your heart, and lean not on your own understanding. (Proverbs 3:5 NKJV)

I did not have a clue what was going on with me! I pulled the lever back on my seat to stretch out. I was in a different world. I stayed there for some time. When I opened my eyes I was all alone in the car. I went to the front door of the house and rang the door bell. The hostess of the potluck let me in and ushered me to sit in the front room. The potluck was over. They had already eaten and were cleaning up. My eyes were adjusting to the dimmer light after coming in from the bright sunlight. I sat down to relax and there at my feet, was a little baby.

I lost my composure and took off. I ended up in a vacant room and Willie was right behind me. I was crying uncontrollably. I didn't understand what was happening to me. Willie said, "George, the Lord is healing your past, your first abortion." I found out later the baby was the youth pastor's son and was only a few weeks old.

As we drove back from the potluck, Mary Jo and Willie started to discuss the coming conference. Mary Jo realized that she had never used the last chapter about the aborted babies in her sermons before. She asked me if I was willing to share my testimony.

The Holy Spirit inside of me said, "Are you willing to be transparent with your sins?" He reminded me again, (Paraphrase, James 5:16 KJV), *Confess your sins to one another and pray, so that you may be healed!* I said to myself, "Only for you, Jesus." And I said, "Yes." to Mary Jo.

I spent a lot of time talking to Jesus. I had not really talked to anyone before about this dark side of my past, let alone to a large group of people. It was a small church, but it was filled to capacity, including the two overflow rooms. The hour arrived; it was my turn to speak. I said to the Lord, *I can do all things through Christ who strengthens me.* (Philippians 4:13 NKJV) Then (Paraphrase, Isaiah 61:1) came to me, *The Spirit of the Lord is upon me and He has anointed me to speak the good news to those who are poor in spirit, to heal the broken hearted and to set the captives free.* As I walked to the podium, I prayed, "Jesus, that is what you came to do and you are still doing it. I ask you to take over now. Thank you. I will give you all the praise and glory. In Your Name I ask it."

As I opened my mouth to speak, the anointing came. I shared my story of having two abortions in the past and how the Lord had orchestrated for me to be at these meetings. I told them that if they could identify with me and have had an abortion, God has mercy and restoration for them. He says in His Word, *If we confess our sins, He is faithful and just to forgive us our sins and cleanse us from all unrighteousness.* (I John 1:9 NKJV)

I spoke about how our imagination can be used to heal our brokenness. The Lord used my imagination to set me free from my first abortion when Willie ministered to me, just the day before. She showed me through prayer how to use my sanctified imagination.

Then I talked about the difference between a sanctified and an unsanctified imagination. I gave (Numbers 13:27, 28, 30, 32 & 33 NIV) as biblical view of an unsanctified imagination:

They gave Moses this account: "We went into the land to which you sent us, and it does flow with milk and honey! Here is its fruit. But the people who live there are powerful, and the cities are fortified and very large."

Then Caleb silenced the people before Moses and said, "We should go up and take possession of the land, for we can certainly do it."

But they did not believe, *but they said, "The land we explored devours those living in it. All the people we saw there are of great size."*

"...We seemed like grasshoppers in our own eyes, and we looked the same to them."

As an example, I spoke about the issue of pornography to illustrate the use of an unsanctified imagination. After the meeting, a young man came up to me and asked for prayer, because he had been convicted of his involvement in pornography and wanted to be set free.

When we were leaving Montana, the Pennington's and Willie wrote words of great encouragement to me in my copy of "6 Big, Big, Big Angels". My life has been enriched by having such wonderful friends. The very last thing that I read was penned by Willie's hand: "George, you are a rare gem of courage. You are so illuminated by His glory. Your journey has only begun. There is so much more for you. This is just a taste. George, you have been set free to set the captives free. Go get 'em George, and don't hold on too tight; you will illuminate dark places and change the destinies of many people. There is no limit. Love, Willie."

I have re-read Willie's words many times for encouragement. It spoke to my heart and confirmed what God was doing and is doing in my life. Restoration and freedom!

Thank you, Jesus!

Chapter 9

Restoration 2009

Three years had gone by since spending the winter in Oregon in the trailer park across the creek from Betty's house. Several friends had encouraged me to talk to her about our abortions. I was willing, but I was not about to show up at her doorstep after being absent from her life for fifty-five years. If it was God's will after all this time, He would have to set it up. I prayed with a friend for the Lord to open the door.

If two of you agree on earth concerning anything that they ask, that it will be done for them, by my father in heaven. (Matthew 18:19 NKJV)

Soon afterwards, I received a phone call from one of my high school friends, telling me that Betty's husband had recently passed away. I felt like this was the open door I had prayed for and felt it was now time to talk to Betty.

I made arrangements to fly to Oregon. When I arrived at the hotel, I began to pray; "Lord, I can do all things through you." And with that I picked up the phone and called Betty.

"Hello, is this Betty?"

"Yes." She replied.

"Hi, this is George Curtiss." I said, "I need to talk to you face to face and want to ask you to forgive me for the anger I had toward you."

"George, that doesn't sound good."

"Betty, it's good. I have good news for you."

With that, we made plans to meet in a mall parking lot the next day.

The next day, as I got into the passenger side of Betty's car, my heart was beating a hundred miles a minute. It had been so very long ago since I had seen Betty, let alone talked to her. I had brought with me the book, "6 Big, Big, Big Angels". I had written down the scriptures in Isaiah that spoke of the babies in the millennium where it took 100 years to grow up, and the letter I had written to my friend, Bill. It went a lot more smoothly than I ever imagined it would. The Lord had prepared the way with His "peace that surpasses all understanding".

...and the peace of God, which surpasses all understanding, will guard your hearts and minds through Christ Jesus. (Philippians 4:7 NKJV)

When I got out of the car to leave, I said, "Betty, I love you in Jesus."

Later that evening my friend, Anne, and I were on our way to a home group meeting, when my cell phone rang; it was Betty. She said, "George, I don't know what is happening to me. I am remembering things I had forgotten all about. My daughter came to visit me and said, 'Mom, what's going on?' I told her that I had just been with an old boy friend. She asked how it went. I told her it went well, and that I couldn't talk about it now, but would tell her about it later."

Again Betty said to me, "I don't know what is happening to me."

I said, "Betty, I know what is happening. The Lord is healing us and setting us free."

She then said, "George, I love you in Jesus, too.

Anne could hear my side of the conversation and when I hung up, she started praising the Lord, and honking the horn. It was truly a time to celebrate!

I called Betty the next day. We talked about so many things; kids, grandkids, etc. It was great to have the freedom just to be able to talk.

It's called RESTORATION. Thank you Jesus for setting us free!

One of the last things Betty said to me was, "George, you need to write a book!

Chapter 10

Field Without Borders

In 2010, when Darlene Hunter called and invited me to be part of the dedication ceremony of their lodge, Susitna River Lodge in Talkeetna, Alaska, she said, "I have you booked for a month to stay with us. You can write your book here." I thought of Moses and Mt. Sinai, which is significant to me. So I called Darlene back and asked if I could stay forty days instead of thirty. I felt that this would be a consecrated time, a time set apart, to allow God to speak to me; to begin to put my story down on paper.

Nathan Lopez led worship for the event. Nathan and I were neighbors when he was a boy and I watched him grow up to become a man of God. It was a special time for me. Nathan had also been asked to be part of the worship team for the Hub Blest Fest Conference in Chicago that October. He invited us all to come and join him there.

One evening after the dedication of the lodge, about four of us watched a movie about a high school couple that had a similar experience as mine. One of the women noticed that this had touched me deeply, so I began to tell my story. She said to me, "George, you need to write about this. I had never seen it from a man's point of view. Maybe I don't own my own body!"

Or do you not know that your body is the temple of the Holy Spirit who is in you, whom you have from God, and you are not your own? For you were bought at a price; therefore glorify God in your body and in your spirit, which are God's. (1 Corinthians 6:19, 20 NKJV)

In October, Darlene, her son Cody, her daughter Annie, and I decided to take Nathan up on his offer and went to the Hub Blest Fest in Chicago. This would be another divine appointment for me. In the very first session, a man came over and sat down beside me. He said, "I usually don't sit this far back, but I saw you in a vision, standing with your mouth open and water dripping into your mouth, but one drop at a time." He continued on, "The heavens opened up above you and a waterfall began to pour out upon you. You put your head back and opened your mouth wide. The Lord said you would have season of refreshing and you were to continue drinking until you were full."

I am the Lord your God, Who brought you out of the land of Egypt; Open your mouth wide, and I will fill it. (Psalm 81:10 (NKJV)

At another session, I was sitting with Cody and Annie when the speaker, Steve Sampson, stopped in the middle of his message and said, "I don't know why I'm saying this, but if there is anyone here who was born in 1933 or about that time, stand up." No one stood up. Cody looked at me. I wasn't born in 1933 but I was born about that time, March 1935. I stood up. Steve then asked me to come up to the front. He then asked if there was anyone who had been in a serious car accident, where they were badly injured, especially a brain injury. Annie and a few others came forward. He said the Lord was going to heal them; and then he said to me, "The Lord is going to add to you ten more good productive years."

After I was called up to the front, I had quite few people come up to speak with me. One of them was a man named Ken. We became fast friends during one of the sessions.

Later in the conference, Cody and Annie came and sat beside me. Annie was crying. She gave me a big hug and whispered that the Lord had healed her completely. She knew she had been healed from the brain and spinal injuries caused from the car accident 10 years earlier. Her leg had grown three inches, her spine had straightened and she had no more pain!

Before the last session, something extraordinary happened. I was in the foyer when I saw a young woman standing there as if she was just waiting for me. We were the only ones there. She approached me and said; "I see you in the middle of a field without borders, ministering!" I was taken aback and said that she had no idea what she just said or how much it meant to me. I couldn't hear any other thing she said. All I continued to hear was the phrase "field without borders, ministering". Later, I tried to find her to talk some more, but I never did see her again the rest of the conference. My thoughts went to (Hebrews 13:2 NKJV) *"Do not forget to entertain strangers, for by so doing some have unwittingly entertained angels."*

This was stranger than fiction, a true confirmation from the Lord! In all His awesome and glorious ways, He confirms with more than one witness. And this was the third witness!

The first witness was in 2008 when I closed my eyes and had the vision of all the aborted babies in heaven. The second one came when I was watching "It's Supernatural" where Sid Roth was interviewing Curtis "Earthquake" Kelly; who had been taken to heaven and had described exactly what I had seen, a beautiful landscape full of children. Now, I knew without a doubt that God was taking care of all the aborted babies and had a plan of redemption for them.

The conference was over, but the Lord had one more miracle to perform.

Our flight back to Anchorage the next day did not leave until late afternoon. My new friend Ken called the next morning. He asked if I would be interested in going with him to see his friend Jack before I left on the plane. He told me that Jack was a veteran, living in a nursing home. He was almost blind and was bedridden. He was a bitter old man that had blamed God for all his problems. I told Ken that I could identify with that, and that I had good news for his friend.

When Ken introduced Jack to me, I said, "The Lord sent me all the way from Alaska to meet you." It was the right introduction to him because he was very interested in Alaska and fishing. I have many fish stories and I shared them with him.

As we talked, Jack expressed how he enjoyed eating smoked trout and how much he loved to fish for trout. I told Jack my oldest son, Troy, was a commercial fisherman. Sometimes he catches steelhead trout in his nets and I would be able to get some smoked trout to him.

That opened the door to Jack's heart for me to share how I had once been a bitter old man and how the Lord was changing my heart of stone into a heart of flesh. I tried the Spirit, and asked Jack if he had ever accepted Jesus when he was a small boy, like maybe in Sunday school. He confessed that he had, but later had lost his faith, when his young son, as well as a cousin had died prematurely. He blamed God for it and wanted nothing more to do with Him.

I shared with him that we could deny Him, but that He could not deny Himself. That He still loved Jack, no matter what. I then repeated how God had sent me all the way from Alaska to tell him that Jesus loves him so much.

If we are faithless, He remains faithful; He cannot deny Himself.
(2 Timothy 2:13 NKJV)

On our way back, Ken said to me that he could see Jack was more peaceful and receptive to the things of the Lord than he had ever seen before. When I got home I sent Jack some smoked fish. Ken phoned me from Jack's bedside as they opened his present from Alaska. Later, Ken shared with me how Jack had changed, how he was telling his family members about Jesus before he passed away.

The Lord had given me two new friends that I would never have to say goodbye to.

"Until we meet again..."

Your Work Is To Believe

We are bought with a price and Jesus paid the price. He restored us back to the Father. It is a free gift. It is called Grace. It is so simple, a child can receive it. We must come as little children with childlike faith. He even gives us the measure of faith to act on it.

Your work is to believe. Just do it! *But as many as received Him, to them He gave the right to become children of God, to those who believe in His name.* (John 1:12 NKJV)

"For God so loved the world that He gave His only begotten Son, that whoever believes in Him should not perish but have everlasting life. For God did not send His Son into the world to condemn the world, but that the world through Him might be saved. He who believes in Him is not condemned; but he who does not believe is condemned already, because he has not believed in the name of the only begotten Son of God." (John 3:16-18 NKJV)

If you have done this, your spirit is born again. Your name is written down in the Lamb's Book of Life, all heaven rejoices and Jesus' Spirit comes to live in you to work out your salvation. He is alive and well, and you can do all things in Him.

I can do all things through Christ who strengthens me. (Philippians 4:13 NKJV)

That's my story and I am sticking to it.

Jesus did many other things. If everyone of them were written down, I suppose that even the whole world would not have room for the books that would be written. (Paraphrase, John 21:25 (NKJV)

What's your story?

CPSIA information can be obtained
at www.ICGtesting.com
Printed in the USA
FFOW02n1551190318
45796639-46682FF